THE LIFE OF A TRAUMA QUEEN

MY ROAD TO REDEMPTION

LaTina Celeste Dorsey, M.A.

ISBN 979-8-88851-948-6 (Paperback)
ISBN 979-8-88851-949-3 (Digital)

Covenant Books
11661 Hwy 707
Murrells Inlet, SC 29576
www.covenantbooks.com

THE TRAUMA BUFFET

*As for you, you meant evil against me, but
God meant it for good in order to bring about this
present outcome, that many people would be kept
alive [as they are this day].*
—Genesis 50:20 AMP

Being sexually abused by my biological father when I was sent to go live with him by my mother because I became too much to deal with.

Listening and enduring the abuse from my biological father, who said to me the reason he wanted to have sex with me was to show me how powerful my vagina area was and that I could use it as a weapon to get whatever I wanted in life.

At the age four or five, being babysat by a second cousin, and he would repeatedly take me into a closet when my mother left, and he would hold me upside down by my ankles with no panties on, and he would masturbate. I remember seeing white, creamy stuff, which later I learned was semen.

Being stabbed in my shoulder blade area of my back after having a physical fight with a female lover. And although that occurred and the relationship was toxic, I stayed, and we tried to still make it work.

Being exposed to oral sex by an older, longtime neighborhood friend, who directed me and a family member to perform oral sexual acts while he watched.

Going days and days without food during my formative school years.

Being bullied in middle school and into my high school years, and being made fun of because everyone knew we had no food to eat and were poor.

Physically looking like someone who lived in a third-world country that suffered from malnutrition because I was so skinny and being taunted and picked on a lot.

Being told by someone I should just go ahead and hang myself and die.

Having to live in a hotel and my vehicle for a period because of being evicted twice.

Being placed on a Greyhound bus and sent to live with my biological father, who was told, "If you don't take her, she is going to a detention home."

Being approached by a half sister, who alluded to having incestuous relations.

Being approached by a first cousin on my biological father's side that offered to me that we get an apartment together and have a sexual relationship, stating that no one would suspect anything because we were cousins.

A failed marriage that ended traumatically.

This list is not exhaustive, and more traumatic encounters will be detailed in further writings of the author of *The Life of a Trauma Queen*.

IT BEGAN BEFORE I
WAS EVEN BORN

*And the LORD passed by before him, and pro-
claimed, "The LORD! The LORD! A God merciful
and gracious, slow to anger, and abundant in lov-
ing-kindness and truth. Keeping mercy and lov-
ing-kindness for thousands, forgiving iniquity and
transgression and sin, but Who will by no means
clear the guilty, visiting the iniquity of the fathers
upon the children and the children's children, to the
third and fourth generation.*
—Exodus 34:6–7 AMP

I always felt like I was slightly different from the other children
that lived in my neighborhood. I was born in a small town called
Sandusky, Ohio, where an amusement park called Cedar Point put
the town on the map. People came—and still do come—from all
over the United States and Canada, bringing their families to visit.
I was the child of a single-parent mom for most of my childhood
life, with an occasional male figure in the picture for short periods
of time. A couple of my mother's partners and/or husbands spent
periods of time in and out of jail. I recall only one, whom my mother
seemed to love deeply, did his best to be a male role model for my
younger brother and me. Although he went to jail many times while
married to my mother, he did try to either directly or indirectly care
for us as a male father would.

He battled drug addiction and usage. His drug of choice was
called "dope," as it was called in those days. My mother did try her

best to raise my younger brother and me the best way she knew how, which was very little because of her fractured, traumatic upbringing. There were three of us born to my biological mother, and we all had different fathers, yet I believed we were close. Somehow, by a series of events, my oldest brother by two years found himself being raised by my great-grandparents. From what I understood, this was common practice that certain children would go away and stay with grandparents and/or other older relatives to help relieve the parenting burden of unwed and, sometimes, unwanted children.

I found out when I was a young adult that my mother was given away to her grandparents because her mother and father thought her to be sickly, and she was labeled or diagnosed by them as having soft bones, along with other ailments. Quite to my surprise, when I was older and was home visiting from the military, my mother's mother showed me a document saying that my mother was "mentally retarded." My mother suffered great rejection, secondary to feeling like her parents did not want her because they never went back to get her and rejoin her back with their family. She watched from afar, with her other siblings being raised by her maternal and paternal parents while she had to live with her grandparents.

It was not until I got older that I came to see that the selection process was not fair because many times, it hinged upon the child's gender and/or condition as to who would take the child in. There were many patterns of dysfunction, abandonment, and rejection that traveled down my family's lineage, and it kept right on traveling until the curse was reversed by way of the blood of Christ Jesus. The seeds of rejection on an emotional level were already a part of my blood and natural DNA, even though I was not consciously aware of it. Rejection had begun her subtle assault into my internal makeup and self-esteem as a child because I was bounced around from house to house when my mother needed someone to babysit me or give me a place to go for the summer.

Exodus 34:7 referenced that iniquity would be visited down to the third and fourth generations, and it was true because of the trauma my biological mother and I suffered as well as my daughter because I viewed myself as being incapable of properly mothering a child. And when my daughter's father and I separated, I wanted her to go live with her father, believing I was too emotionally broken to be a good mother. I suffered great shame because of the many traumatic events that had occurred to me during my beginning years, and I really believed my daughter would be better off without me and that someone else could love and provide for her better.

HAVING A PREDATOR
FOR A FATHER

Although my father and my mother have forsaken me, yet the LORD will take me up adopt me as His child.

—Psalm 27:10 AMP

My biological father was considered a rolling stone, as they called him the type of man back in those days. The meeting of my biological father and mother was something to hear whenever my mother recounted how she followed behind him from show to show because he was a popular local musician and was known for his way with the ladies. I lived with my mother for most of my school years but was sent/forced to go and live with my biological father and my stepmother when I was in the tenth grade. My father possessed an incestuous spirit that traveled down from his father (my grandfather), and who knows how far back through the ancestral line it went. My father was tall, dark, and handsome, and women flocked to him and literally were easy sexual partners for him.

When I went to live with my father, I really thought I was being rescued somehow and that he would make my life better, but it was quite the opposite. He was a friendly man and was very funny, and people loved to be around him. However, behind closed doors, he was a pedophile, to say the least. There were accounts of my biological father having sexual relations with several of my half sisters, but no one came out about it publicly.

When I reached the age of seventeen years old, I decided to try and get away on the first locomotive smoking from them, and

I joined the military. Needless to say, my perception and feelings toward men were very twisted from what my biological father did to me and the males through my early childhood years. Many people judged me and criticized me because I couldn't stomach a man having what I considered was power over me through the vehicle of their penis. When God came for me and pursued me relentlessly, I became open to the love of Him, His Son, Christ Jesus, and the Holy Spirit.

It took many years of trauma recovery by becoming intentionally knowledgeable in the understanding of trauma, trauma bonds, trauma repression, trauma triggers, trauma symptoms, and the devastation that trauma could leave behind to pass on to your offspring, even when you didn't really realize it. During my academic pursuits in the field of trauma, I learned a couple of key facts regarding traumatic impact. One that our very cells hold memory, so even when years past and various traumas may be far removed from our conscious mind, our cells will respond when the effects of the traumatic injury are triggered in even the slightest way. There can be a lot of reliving of traumatic events in an individual's present life.

For many years, and even decades in fact, I could not stomach a man's touch, let alone his penis penetration. However, there were times that I occasionally desired physical satisfaction from the male's body part of his penis but not so much him as the man. I just wanted to satisfy my physical, erotic urges. As I grew in understanding of what I was really after, I realized that I desired intimacy—true intimacy from someone. After several failed relationships with mostly women, I determined that what I was looking for was not going to be found in a human.

There is a void, a hole within each of us that longs for deep filling, and that can only come through a reunion with the Maker of us all. His name is Jehovah, *Yahweh*, the *Great I Am*, and a host of other powerful descriptive ascribing *words*. I'm so grateful the God of the universe adopted me and made me His precious own through His Son, Christ Jesus, because this has been the foundational stability and strength in all domains of my existence, that is, psychologically, emotionally, relationally, and physically.

LIVING LIKE A NOMAD

To this hour we have gone both hungry and thirsty, we habitually wear but one undergarment and shiver in the cold; we are roughly knocked about and wander around homeless.
—1 Corinthians 4:11 AMP

I have nothing but respect for the homeless population that, in spite of not having a place to call home on a consistent basis, they keep getting back up each day and trying to make the best of what they have and where they are in life. However, the psychology of the matter is that when an individual doesn't have a stable home and access to the basic necessities of life—like clean water for drinking and bathing, heat, and structural shelter to protect from the various elements of weather and dangers and a place to rest—and can't refresh themselves, they are more prone to suffer from things such as anxiety, depression, and, sometimes, substance usage. In my adult years, I experienced a form of homelessness when I was evicted and had to live in a hotel and out of my vehicle. This sense of displacement pierced me deeply because of all the bouncing around I experienced as child and during my high school years when I was forced to go live with my biological father and his family.

I grew up living like a *nomad*. I lived most of my younger years with my mother, but we moved a lot. We also moved from city to city, which produced a greater level of instability with regard to healthy childhood attachments because we had to start over again and again, trying to build bonds with both adults and childhood friends. I recall being dropped off at various houses to be babysat by either relatives or some of my mother's acquaintances/friends. I remember always severely crying whenever my mother would drop me off at an older lady's house, who lived across the street from my great-grandfather, to watch over me.

From the stories my grandmother told me, my younger brother and I weren't well taken care of by my mother, nor were we fed properly. According to my grandmother, our diet consisted of hot dogs and beans when we did have food. It's interesting how children don't know they are neglected or poorly being taken care of unless someone else tells them. Children, for the most part, just want to be with their parents, and they believe, by default, that their parents love them, which is not the case.

Because I was bounced around so much by either being sent away for the summers or being cared for by random relatives and friends during the school year, I was exposed to many inappropriate experiences and viewings. One of the most vivid sexual trauma experiences I remember is when an older cousin would take me into a closet and hold me upside down, with no panties on, and he would masturbate. I referenced this in the first chapter because, although I don't remember any physical penetration such as what my biological father did to me, the sexual trauma experienced by such repeated behavior proved to be deeply disturbing to me as a female.

DESPERATELY WANTING TO BE LOVED

For God so [greatly] loved and dearly prized the world, that He [even] gave His [One and] [a] only begotten Son, so that whoever believes and trusts in Him [as Savior] shall not perish but have eternal life.

—John 3:16 AMP

I became intentionally sexually active at the age of fourteen when I was living with my mother and my youngest brother. I used to hang out with the west-side children into all times of the evening, riding bikes, mopeds, listening to music, smoking weed, and drinking forty ounces of beer. I recall wanting to fit in so bad and to feel normal that I would do just about anything to feel a sense of belongingness. There were a couple of boys that made me feel as if I could only be accepted if I became sexually active with them. I decided on one boy, who was several years older than me, to engage sexually with. I learned a huge lesson after I engaged with him sexually, and that was that he had a big mouth and ran and told everyone we knew no sooner than the sexual intercourse was done. I felt even greater shame about myself after that situation occurred.

The continued sexual trauma I endured with men since as far back as I could remember began to take a toll on my sexual identity. I believe it was during my middle school years that I wondered if I was heterosexual or not. My mother was emotionally absent and barely physically present because she was trying to live herself the best way she knew how. My mother struggled with knowing how to parent any children in a healthy way because she experienced a very difficult relationship with her mother. My biological mother did give us a physical home and, for the most part, provided clothes for me and my youngest brother to wear. However, there was neglect present in many other ways, such as going many days without food to eat.

After surviving my emotionally, mentally, and sexually traumatic childhood years, I was able to escape by enlisting into the military. I remember I visited my mother when I was an adult and confronted her about my experiences as a child, and she denied it all and became angry. I left her house angry and stopped speaking to her for many years. I learned that accountability is something most people don't readily embrace. Actually, she nor my biological father wanted to be held accountable for their actions and contributions to the many traumatic experiences I encountered while in their care. I remember confronting my father as well when I came home on a military liberty pass, and he stopped speaking to me because I told what he did to me to many people in our town plus the family. I found out years later that he had molested pretty much all the females who were his offspring. However, I am not aware if he performed any incestuous acts on the males in his household or other children, but I did find out that his incestuous spirit and behavior came down through his father—my grandfather.

As I gained the courage to not just confront my abusers but even confront my past and the things that happened to me, I became accountable to myself and became engendered with a desire to be better and to be something more than the passed-around throwaway that I felt like. I became accountable, little by little, by seeking understanding and healing and, ultimately, by overcoming the traumatic devastations that crippled my life, and my ability to love, receive love, and be mentally sound.

My father died many years ago, but I realize that had my telling what he did to me was told to a mandated reporter, he would have been investigated and perhaps jailed. I am amazed at how many people keep such inappropriate and horrific acts a secret within the family, and they slowly die from within from holding it in and acting like things didn't happen. The secrecy impacts their mental health on some very deep levels emotionally, psychologically, and, oftentimes, physically as they are plagued by pain and many mental health disorders. I experienced a lot of pain, maladaptive thoughts, and behaviors because of the trauma I experienced for many years.

JUST TRYING
TO SURVIVE

My physical appearance was like that of someone living in a third-world country because of how skinny and malnourished I was growing up. I used to try to earn money by doing things like getting a paper route, etc. so I could buy food. However, such endeavors didn't last very long for whatever reason I couldn't recall. I do know I attempted to strategize that if I could earn enough money to buy things like Snickers, candy bars, and other junk food, I would not starve to death. I recall experiencing a lot of disassociation growing up when I would just leave many present moments of consciousness and would have a daze come over me. I thought it was just something I did, but during the attaining of my master's degree in trauma/crisis response, I then understood that it was a post-traumatic stress symptom.

Living as a Black female within this country was traumatic all by itself. As a little Black girl growing up enduring various forms of trauma, I was just trying to survive. I recall very few role models I wanted to be like. There was one elementary school teacher that seemed to treat me as her own. I remember being in sixth grade and staying overnight with her and her family on some weekends. She was a Black female who didn't take any stuff from her students or anyone, yet she had a very open heart for children like me I suppose. I use to get so excited, knowing I would be able to stay overnight at my teacher's home and be treated good.

As I progressed into my middle school years, I recall daydreaming a lot and fantasying a lot about being someone else's child. From the outside looking, the few friends I had seemed to be well taken care of. They had plenty of food to eat, and they had parents who gave them money to do what they wanted. I remember living a very embarrassing life and feeling great shame because many of my peers and their parents knew that we didn't have food to eat oftentimes. I find it interesting how many people knew of my home life, but no one said anything or seemed to care enough to initiate any form of intervention. However, perhaps they did, and I knew nothing about it. And now that I think of it, I can see that the elementary teacher who took me under her wing and went above and beyond just being my sixth-grade teacher was an intervention of sorts because I had a safe place to go, food to eat, and I felt a part of decently functioning family.

REJECTED AND FORSAKEN

For He has said I will never [under any circumstances] desert you [nor give you up nor leave you without support, nor will I any degree leave you helpless], nor will I forsake or let you down or relax my hold on you [assuredly not]!
—Hebrews 13:5 AMP

From as far back as I remember, I had always felt severely rejected by everyone and anyone I came into contact or relationship with. The constant and prolonged trauma and abuse in various forms impacted me in such a way that I did not believe anyone would want to love me or have me around once they found out about my experiences and my tainted past. Rejection and the feelings of it constantly paralyzed me socially, and I spent many of my years feeling isolated and alone. I thought I would be safe emotionally and mentally behind the walls I erected, where I believed no one could ever hurt me again. After functioning like this for a long period of time, I did not know how to function in basic intimate relationships or friendships of any kind. However, it was interesting that people, both men and women, were always drawn toward me.

During my young adult years, I began to notice I went from having some affection toward men to basically none at all. I was nauseated wherever I saw women chasing after men all the time, even when they were being cheated on and treated very poorly. I saw so much of this growing up by the women in my community, and I also saw how women were treated like nothing more than sexual objects.

I reached a place where I could not tolerate a man penetrating me in any capacity, emotionally and definitely not physically.

At seventeen years of age, I went into the military. I joined the United States Marine Corps, which was considered one of the roughest branches of the military to go into, but I did not care because of how desperately I wanted to get away from what seemed like living in the twilight zone. During my years in the military was when I first realized how very angry and prone I was to severe acts of aggression. Nonetheless, I found, at least for a time, a place where I felt like I belonged, even though there was a good amount of prejudicial activity going on toward Black military personnel. I became hard as nails emotionally and rarely cried. I reached a point during my military years where I don't think I ever cried, and if I saw anyone cry, even a child, it would enrage me. I learned to "suck it up and keep it moving" as they say, which was just another way to say I suppressed all feelings. And by all accounts I did, just that to the point of repressing memories of the traumatic experiences I endured for a couple of decades. I mingled and had some good guy friends throughout all my early adult years, but I didn't find any of them attractive.

AN ANGEL ALONG
THE WAY

For He will command His angels in regard to you, to protect and defend and guard you in all your ways [of obedience and service]. They will lift you up in their hands, So that you do not [even] strike your foot against a stone.
—Psalm 91:11–12 AMP

As I look back at how I somehow ended up in the United States Marine Corps, I believe it had to be a divine intervention that God provided as a way of escape from the abuse and psychological, emotional, sexual, and physical trauma I had experienced for most of my life. Although I was a scared and timid Black girl, I still stepped out forward and joined. It was one of the most pivotal life decisions I ever made. The Marine Corps was, by no means, a walk in the park as they say, but it truly satisfied a longing to be a part of something that would transport me from where I was mentally, emotionally, and even physically by letting me get away. My oldest brother of two years had enlisted in the Army, and, for all accounts and purposes, I thought that I would go that route. However, when I went to the military recruiters building in my small town, the United States Army Recruiter was not there. As I walked down the hall, out popped a sharp, squared-away-looking Marine recruiter, and he said something like, "Hey there, let me talk to you." I believe that Marine Corps recruiter was a divine door en route to a series of new doors that would lead me to where I am today.

Prior to joining the Marine Corps, I went back to stay with my mother for the summer months before being shipped to basic training at Paris Island in South Carolina. While temporarily staying with my mother again, I met a middle-aged African American lady that was a relative of one of my mother's good friends. She had such a kind spirit about her and a beautiful glow unlike I had seen in other church people. She seemed to genuinely care about me, and I felt an immediate sense of trust toward her and whenever I was around her. She took me to church during those summer months before being shipped off to basic training. And that was when I had my first true spiritual awakening. During one of the services I attended with her, I gave my life to Christ Jesus. I remember standing up and sharing with the congregation my name, and I also shared with them that I would soon be shipped off to basic training. I naively believed that I was invincible because of how empowered I felt when I experienced that glorious spiritual new birth.

Whenever I ponder what was different about the lady who profoundly impacted my life before I went out into the world on my own, I know it is because she had a *different* spirit about her. Up to this point in my life, my experiences within the church and with church people were bland and dull although we in our culture have been known to shout and sing loudly and also raise the righteous roof, so to speak. I do not mean these things in a disrespectful way toward my culture because the truth is, the Black church has been a strength to many of my people and to communities everywhere when there is a need for rallying together.

ANGRY AND EXPLOSIVE

Wrath is cruel and anger is an overwhelming flood.
—Proverbs 27:12 AMP

I entered the United States Marine Corps emotionally broken, scared, and angry all at the same time. I turned eighteen years old while I was in basic training, also known as boot camp. I remember vividly being bused onto the island with other females in the wee hours of the night. It was so black outside that you couldn't really see how the bus got on the island. Marine Corps boot camp was an experience I will never forget. The Marine Corps became my parent because it showed me all the things I was never taught growing up. I learned how to adapt and overcome and accomplish just about anything I set my mind to, and it taught me how to destroy whatever was deemed an adverse enemy or threat.

Some of the biggest and most lasting traits that the Marine Corps taught and developed in me were a sense of teamwork, discipline, passion, courage, and perseverance. I attribute these traits that I have been graced with as ultimately coming by way of the grace of God. I still possess these virtuous strengths and graces, and I know that they have been foundational to getting me where I am today, both personally and professionally. I have traveled many rough roads psychologically, emotionally, physically, relationally, financially, and otherwise, but having the mental resilience to still press forward and persevere were strengths I attribute that God blessed me with. And He used my Marine Corps experience to excellently harness and flip the negative adverse trauma I had endured into a channel of positive productivity that launched me forward in life.

However, as I progressed through my military years, I realized my anger had rage underlying it. I found myself in toxic relations with others, and if anything triggered my insecurities or feelings of inadequacy, I would literally become enraged and attack verbally and sometimes, physically. I must admit that it was only the grace of God that kept me alive and did not allow me to be locked up for many years or for the rest of my life for being involved in intimate partner violence. The rage I felt during most of my military years was overlooked for the most part because Marines are classified as being very aggressive by nature, and I had even heard being labeled crazy. Marines have also been known to be called devil dogs, which suggests they are vicious because devil dogs have such characteristics. I presently don't identify with such a descriptive term because of my conversion to Christ Jesus, coupled with my spiritual growth, maturity, and emotional/psychological healing, but I admit I was vicious in all senses of the word for many years of my adult life. My rage and anger were so bad that I was ordered to anger management classes while serving in the Marine Corps.

Interestingly though, my natural temperament would be classified as an introvert, so I didn't go looking to destroy anything, but if a situation presented to me in any adverse or hostile manner, it seemed as though I would go into a trance, and an automated rage response would be triggered, and the only thing on my mind was to take out or down the perceived threat to me physically, mentally, or emotionally. And to be frank, I had one focus, and that was to destroy what I thought could pose a harm to me by any means necessary. The key word is *perceived* because of what I learned through my extensive trauma healing, education, and training. I would become stuck in erroneous thought patterns that always seemed to play out the exact same traumatic story line. I believe I developed post-traumatic stress yet was never officially diagnosed with it. However, I was categorized as having great anxiety and other adjustment challenges.

From my professional training and academic advancement in the arena of trauma, I believe I got overlooked somehow because my responses to situations, people, and circumstances fit such criteria according to APA guidelines for having PTSD. During a couple of my military years, I did have the opportunity to attend a couple of counseling sessions while serving in the military, but nothing of a prolonged duration and nothing that I remember had lasting therapeutic effects on my life. As I look back on those years, I am forever grateful that I was blessed and fortunate to gain an honorable discharge because my state of behavior and presentation was extremely rough, to say the least. I believed in God during my military years and would pray occasionally, but I did not have a true relationship with Christ Jesus until some years after I was discharged and after my life had literally hit rock bottom. I found no reason to keep trying and really didn't want to live because of how dissatisfied I was with life, and I was very tired of hurting inside.

MY PERSONAL LIFE

There seemed to be a glimmer of light when I met my daughter's father. My journey through the military afforded me the opportunity to connect with a man, who I felt had a gentle spirit, yet he was very much a man. We became friends and started hanging out, going places together, working out, doing physical exercises, and such. He was a gifted athlete and played for the Marine Corps basketball team. We eventually became romantically involved and decided to try to see where things would go with us. I realized I came to like and admire him because he was different from many of the Black men I was used to encountering in the world, who seemed more interested in smashing, that is, having sex with a woman than getting to know her as a person. Even though he was coming out of a relationship when we began our involvement, it was the closest thing to perfect with a man I had ever encountered.

Our relationship moved into marriage, and a daughter was born secondary to our union. As I reflect back on the years I was blessed to be married, I have no regrets because I was able to experience the birth of a beautiful daughter, who is now grown, married, and the mother of my many grandchildren. During the marriage, I realized that the effects of my past trauma scarred me so deeply emotionally and psychologically that I was in no shape to be an adequate wife or mother. I became divorced because of being an emotional wreck and displaying very destructive behaviors that simply did not foster any type of healthy relationship. I no longer had affection for my husband, and I suffered from extreme shame because I believed I failed him, my daughter, and myself.

There was a repeated recording in my thoughts that told me I was unfit as a mother and that my daughter would be better off without me. I believed these thoughts, and I chose to let my daughter stay with her biological father. My years of separation from my daughter were very traumatic for me mentally, even though I had joint legal custody of our daughter when her father and I separated and divorced. I experienced an intense desire to try to protect her from experiencing sexual abuse like what I had suffered through my childhood years. My thoughts became irrational, and my behavior reflected it. I experienced many dreams during those years where in the dreams, I was always going to where my daughter was and literally physically destroying anyone I thought would hurt my daughter. I trusted no one.

MY SEXUAL APPETITE

Run away from sexual immorality [in any form, whether thought or behavior, whether visual or written]. Every other sin that a man commits is outside the body, but the one who is sexually immoral sins against his own body.

Childhood sexual trauma is a very ugly thing to endure. The effects of the gross trauma I experienced as early as three years old twisted my sense of the pure, proper, and appropriate. I saw, at a very early age, women performing sexual acts with women and more than two people having sexual relations at one time. I experienced such an act with two adults—a man and a woman, both in their thirties. I believe that act opened me up to have a deeper desire for women. My sexual identity became very blurred and confusing, but I did not believe I could talk to anyone about it. I do know that I looked at both Black men and Black women differently. I began to despise weak Black women who did just about anything to have a man in their life. I saw women chasing after men that they knew were cheating on them, yet they stayed with them and allowed the infidelity to continue as long as that man came home to them.

As I moved through my twenties, thirties, and forties, I developed a hunger for the touch of another woman. It wasn't so much the sexual engagement with a woman that appealed to me, but it was the intimacy and internal closeness with a woman that satisfied me greatly. After several failed same-sex relationships, I decided to just leave things alone in terms of striving to develop a personal romantic relationship. I realized that what I was looking for and/or in need of was not going to be found in another woman or human for that matter. I remember praying to God on several occasions during my searching and yearning years to take away my desire for women. It seemed like He didn't do it right away but healed me and delivered me from my traumatic romantic tendencies a little at a time. As I allowed and accepted God's love for me and began to trust Him, my traumatized soul and mind healed, but it took a couple of decades for me to experience such a complete deliverance and healing from the severe complex trauma I endured throughout my childhood and adult years.

MY FIRST RESPONDER YEARS

After serving for almost eleven years with the Baltimore County Fire Department, I decided, after much prayer and pondering, to move on professionally. This decision came after several of my last years functioning as a paramedic with the fire department and not having the sense of the purposed peace that I once knew while serving with them. I have nothing but good things to say about the Baltimore County Fire Department because it truly changed my life, both professionally and personally. I entered their fire academy and successfully completed the necessary training and medical academic component necessary to become a recognized emergency medical technician, basic for the jurisdiction of Baltimore County.

I quickly moved through the ranks, and within two and a half years, I was promoted to the classification of a paramedic after reentering their fire academy to undergo the necessaries on both national and state levels to function as a paramedic. And although I left the ranks of the department, I have been both blessed and fortunate to maintain an active paramedic license, secondary to meeting the necessary national and state requirements. I will always be grateful for the opportunity that I had to serve with some of the finest men and women on the front lines of community service within Baltimore County. For the most part, there were no Black or White racial issues outwardly, but during many of the years, the sting of prejudicial behavior was seen and felt by multiple African Americans such as me, who served within the department. It was personally disheartening to know that some of my brethren of different race would do things to try to keep people, who were not within the "good ole boy" network, down or from professionally advancing unless you were willing to play the political games some in leadership presented. However, I am grateful that I didn't take a total disliking to the Caucasians I served with because I did have several of them that took me under their wing and watched out for me, and I greatly appreciated it.

I served under the leadership of an awesome captain when I was sent to my first fire station right out of the academy, and I know that God used his demeanor and genuine caring for his personnel to change my perspective regarding White males. I also had a very fair and kind battalion chief that I served under while I was in the department. His leadership and fairness maintained me literally, especially when I was falsely accused by a junior person I worked with of inappropriate behavior. The individual was a Black female, which made it all the more horrific to endure. I had suffered some of the cruelest things from people in my own race and not just from Caucasians. And when all the events occurred in this country, secondary to Mr. George Floyd's wrongful death, I did not jump on that bandwagon as if all White police officers are bad. There are good and bad in all races, and I have experienced such, both in the professional sector as well as in my personal dealings.

However, I did struggle greatly with the feelings that I had toward many of the up-and-coming White males within the fire department because they seemed to move and operate with a sense of entitlement. And their behavior was often reinforced by some of the department's senior leadership. There were many occasions where I felt almost paranoid being around many of the White males within the department because you never knew who knew who and who didn't like you for whatever reason. I believe many of the reasons were what was known as a type of profiling and/or stereotyping of Black females or Blacks in general. However, God being God, He could not allow me to lump whole groups of people into a racially biased category as evil or bad. As I have grown in my faith as well as in my understanding of humanity as a whole, I know that it's a humanity thing, and that there are more deep-seated biases, prideful postures, and bigotry that run in the blood of mankind as a whole that need more addressing than just a Black or White thing.

MY MENTAL HEALTH

For several of my years functioning with the fire department, I suffered from severe bouts of depression and anxiety, secondary to having such a great responsibility for other people's lives, which included men, women, children, and even infants at times. The role and responsibilities of a paramedic are far-reaching when it comes to having the ability to medically influence if someone would have the greatest opportunity to live or die in acute medical and sometimes mental circumstances that they found themselves in. The trauma that first responders are exposed to presupposes the occupations to be hazardous on many levels, and I can say that is very true. I have not only endured many types of trauma myself, such as being stabbed in the upper part of my back by a lover during our frequent intimate partner violence eruptions, but I was also involved in violent destructive behavior that hurt other people and that destroyed property.

Somehow, even during those years, I knew enough to pray and ask God to help me make it through and to get out of the relational entanglements I found myself in. I realized, after going through a few failed toxic personal relationships, that what drew or attracted me to certain types of people, particularly females, was that we shared what was called *trauma bonds*. Even though many of my years in personal relationships were crippled by toxicity, intimate partner violence, anger, and destruction, I was still graced to function professionally at a high caliber, which saved and/or assisted thousands of individuals, in one way or another, to move from their crisis—mentally, emotionally, or physically—to a state of calm or stabilization. It was during my first responder years that I began to grasp I could be so much more than what my traumatic history and past etched in my mind deemed I could be.

MY WAY OUT

During my many years of searching for love, meaning, and truth, I have found that nothing and no one had the ability to stabilize my mind mentally, emotionally heal me, or purposefully reset me and then give me divine direction to my life but God. And although during my seemingly successful climb from a throwaway, rejected, and abused little Black girl, who somehow was able to miraculously maintain a focus and determination to attain her master's degree in trauma/crisis response, I was still terribly broken from the inside out, and I could no longer fix myself or cover up things and keep moving as I had done for the last several decades while helping many people and also intervening into people's lives, both personally and professionally, keeping them from killing themselves literally. The truth is I paid little attention to fixing myself but was merely bandaging my traumatic wounds. In my mind, I felt they did not need my attention because "Hey, I served in the United States Marine Corps" and I adhered to the saying "You just suck it up, Marine" and continued on conquering whatever posed an obstacle to my life's objectives by any means necessary. Well, little did I know that *by any means necessary* was at the expense of my mental, emotional, and physical health.

So upon entering my doctoral studies in 2019, right before the deadly virus COVID-19 hit the world, my life apexed, and I ran out of gas—so to speak—strength, and a reason to live. I cried out to God from a state of despair because my life had completely fell apart personally, relationally, and financially. Prior to my life reaching the place of climatic breakdown, I thought I was leaving my profession as a full-time first responder for purely educational-pursuing reasons, which was not the case. I realized later that I was internally prompted by the spirit of Christ Jesus to leave that I might not completely die

29

mentally, emotionally, physically, and spiritually. Life had taken its destructive toll on me in all domains of my existence, and I could no longer repress my traumatic past or avoid it. My body became grossly ill, and I suffered from severe hemorrhaging. I experienced female hormonal imbalances, where I became in need of several blood transfusions. I had been bleeding heavily for many years and developed fibroids and other maladies that had the potential to assist me in leaving this Earth expeditiously.

As I begin to descend in terms of the closing of the writing of my first book, I want to spend the last portion of it expressing to you and assuring you that you are not alone and that God sees you, *loves* you, and has provided a *way* out for you. And all that you might have suffered traumatically or otherwise from childhood into your adulthood, He has been aware of it. Many people struggle with trying to understand how a loving God could allow them to suffer and/or endure what they had. The answer is both simple and yet complex at the same time. Yes, if the God of the Bible is who He says He is, then why didn't He step in then or even now in my circumstances and the traumatic circumstances of others? My response to you is simply this: that He did step in when He sent His only begotten Son, Christ Jesus, into the world to not only seek, but also to save the lost mentally, the shattered emotionally, and the psychologically destroyed because of the horrific trauma they suffered from. He loved the world so much and His creation that He allowed His Son Jesus Christ to come from glory, where He resided in the heavenlies, and be born through a woman, to live, to be an example, to love, to be detained, to be beaten beyond recognition, to be mocked, to be spit upon, to be pierced in His side, to have a crown of thorns placed on His head and then to die for all of mankind.

Many people or other religious groups refute what the Bible states, and that is there is only one way to God. Jesus Christ said about Himself, "I am the [only] Way [to God] and the [real] Truth and the [real] Life; no one comes to the Father but through Me" (John 14:6 AMP). Jesus Christ paid the ultimate price by giving His life for every human's sins and that includes those that have inflicted trauma on you in any way. And once I came to terms with the fact that even though I had a lot of bad stuff happen to me, I had done what would be considered a lot of bad stuff to others. I learned through my broken season of 2019 and into 2020 that I had no legal grounds to hold unforgiveness and hatred and to be bitter toward anyone.

God has kept record of every one of our sins and wrongs committed, whether intentionally or unintentionally, and He alone, because He is sovereign, can mete out what is owed to who and how much regarding grace, mercy, or punishment. I am so grateful for a loving God, who knows how to take what was meant to destroy me, turned it around, flipped my condemned house/me, and caused me to become a beautiful dwelling with a God-inspired mission to track, trace, teach, and assist Him in rescuing the countless others still traumatized by their experiences.

THE EFFECTS
OF TRAUMA

We are three-part beings that comprise of a spirit, soul, and body, and when trauma has occurred to any part of our being, the other parts of us will be affected in one way or another. My spiritual awakening to the *truth* found in the Word of God concerning what this life is all about and how to heal and/or correct any part of my existence has been the greatest treatment modal I have personally utilized, along with self-administered, cognitive behavioral and cognitive processing therapies. However, this may not be the approach for others, and there are many psychotherapies available for one to consider with a therapist as part of a client-centered treatment plan. So please keep that in mind as you consider your trauma recovery options.

As I pursued my educational goals and became more knowledgeable with the topic of trauma and its effect on a person, I realized how deep traumatic experiences and injury can really go. I won't go into the science of trauma per se, but I will share with you that the very cells of our body hold memory, and if trauma has been inflicted on an individual in any way—emotionally, mentally, or physically—then that traumatic experience has the potential to affect how a person will subconsciously and sometimes consciously respond to things in their life, whether or not it is readily seen or expressed. As a child, I experienced various traumatic experiences that put my development emotionally, relationally, and mentally into a fractured developmental category.

Trauma, at its base definition, is known as a wound or very distressing and/or very disturbing experience that someone or something has suffered. Childhood sexual trauma, abuse, and rape suffered at an early age provide an inroad for many personality disorders and identity challenges that I know many of our youth in the world face. I also learned and have experienced while working with a mental health agency that suicidal thoughts and suicidal ideation are greatly connected to individuals experiencing childhood trauma and events. During my attaining of my master's degree in trauma/crisis response, I had the opportunity to take many required classes that went into depth regarding how trauma opens doors to many mental health challenges and disorders, such as post-traumatic stress disorder (PTSD), acute stress disorder (ASD), personality disorders, and attachment disorders. Oftentimes, children are misdiagnosed or not diagnosed until well in their years post the trauma suffered by them.

Unstable homes can produce unstable children but not always. Historically, when people think of homelessness, they think of adults being the population referenced, but there are more and more children living on the street, in abandoned buildings, or in other unsafe dwelling that expose them to greater cycles of abuse, sex trafficking, and exploitation of all kinds. Although my home life was very unstable because I was bounced around from house to house like I was in foster care, I did not have to be what is considered fully homeless. I do remember having to stay overnight at my grandfather's house on one occasion, and I went into a panic state and ran out of the house in the middle of the night, knocking on doors and randomly asking for help. My family was located, and I then had to live with various families that would take me in until I had to go live back with my biological father.

As an adult, I experienced a form of homelessness after being evicted from an apartment, and I had to live in a hotel for a period of about nine months. I lived out of my car as well. I remember having a dazed look and an awfully empty feeling in the pit of my stomach because whenever the sun went down, I knew I would not have a home to go to. But God kept me and who I was with that we did not have to resort to illegal activity or the selling of bodies.

There are many people I know that have had to resort to such activity, and that has had a deep impact on them mentally, emotionally, and psychologically. The shame and guilt associated with such activity has eroded their sense of worth and esteem on levels that many could never understand unless an individual experienced such. Many have been raped and traumatically assaulted by being exposed to unsafe environments because of the risk associated with them trying to make money to survive. Without intervention, the trauma trap perpetuates itself in an individual's life and can multiply, causing greater mental instability. I am grateful that God kept my mind stable enough to make it through. I recall having suicidal thoughts when I was living with my biological father and the devastation I felt having the man, who was supposed to protect me, penetrating me sexually and trying to explain it away as his way of teaching me how valuable my vagina was and that I could use it as a weapon of power to get ahead in life.

MY PASSION, PURPOSE, AND PURSUIT

I came from nothing, so to speak. I was written off by *MANY*, whether relationally, personally, and mentally. By the grace of God, I was able to come *up*, OUT, and *through* my extensive trauma that was inflicted in areas of my life. The love of God and His pursuit of me in a relentless manner has caused me to now be passionate with regard to reaching others. As I have been given, I am to freely give according to the Word of God. I am quite aware that there are millions of Latinas out there in the world, both male and female, still suffering from present trauma or from past traumatic experiences that have dismantled them from the inside out.

My academic accomplishments in terms of attaining a master's degree in trauma and crisis response afforded me a deeper look at how trauma affects a person. My present academic involvement with striving to attain a doctoral degree has given me an even greater ability to not just understand the complexities of trauma mentally, emotionally, psychologically, and physically, but become part of the healing process for the countless individuals that cross my path in a professional setting through my consulting firm Forward Focus & Recovery Consulting LLC or through my function as an elder at my church. I did not know that when I decided to finish my bachelor's degree in crisis counseling and psychology when I was still functioning as a paramedic with the Baltimore County Fire Department, my thirst for more learning and expertise in trauma would take me to where I am today. However, as I have gotten to know God, the Most High, Jehovah, the Great I Am, I have come to experience and realize that He does *all* things well. The dots of my life, my purpose, and my destiny have taken a formative image of what overcoming great adversity looks like in the face of great odds beginning at birth.

I have found that my purpose is connected to everything I have suffered in my life, whether at the hands of others or my own poor choices. I mention the part concerning my own poor choices because I believe it is important to note that I am not, nor was I, perfect in everything I have done. Oftentimes, people who have suffered from abuse or being violated in any form feel justified for their present actions and decisions. The spirit of accountability is loosely embraced by many, who do not want to face or confront their past or their present. What I do know is that patterns of behavior, whether destructive, deviant, or negative, have their root, and many times, the learned behavior was passed down from somewhere or someone an individual has had contact with. However, it is not okay to just go along with the program, so to speak, and do to others what has been done to you, especially if the behavior or words you use are belittling, violent, and/or abusive.

I am not sure when or how I realized that I was no longer a victim to what had happened to me by some in my family, who were supposed to nurture, guide, and teach me how to live life, but I am forever grateful that a change came over me and into me, stimulating me to do whatever was necessary to be victorious. And even now, I hold no malice toward anyone that intentionally abused me or neglected me and did not provide the necessities I needed to grow because I understand that people can't give you what they do not have. I did have more of a struggle with forgiving my now deceased biological father because of the devastating impact of his incestuous acts with me, but God has given me the ability—after many years of healing and gaining understanding of many spiritual matters, such as iniquitous transference, mental health strongholds, and other things—that I have no connection internally or otherwise to what he deliberately did to me. I have been healed, delivered, and set free from all the residue that he deposited in my spirit, soul, emotions, and mind. And God the Father and Creator of all mankind has become my true spiritual Father and covering. He has provided me all I need through people, both males and females, along my life's journey that filled in the gaps I had in various forms.

My biological mother is still alive, and I am very grateful that we have had an opportunity to restore our mother-daughter relationship, even though I sometimes feel that I will never experience certain things with her now that I am an adult. I was able to gain insight into her struggles as a child, the verbal abuse she incurred from her mother, and how it literally caused her to feel like a dog. I use the term *dog* as a description of how she felt internally from hearing how she would reference herself many times because of the way people did or tried to treat her. It's interesting how abuse incurred and, over a long period of time, has the great potential to erode one's sense of worth and esteem. I experienced these things myself, where words spoken to me and things done to me left me feeling insecure, with low self-esteem, and lacking in feelings of self-worth.

I speak nothing ill about my mother's mother because she died, but I do know that I witnessed her speaking very destructively to my mother while I was present. I recall one time I was visiting home on military leave, and I went to visit my grandmother to be cordial, and when I entered her home, she thought I was my mother and yelled obscenities to me. When I corrected her, she apologized. I then went on to share with my grandmother that she should not speak to my mother like that and that it was inappropriate. It greatly angered me, which didn't take much in those days because I hadn't healed or been delivered of my explosive anger issues. She did settle down, and during the conversation, for whatever reason, she felt she needed to show me a document she kept near her that stated my mother was supposedly classified "mentally retarded." I was absolutely flabbergasted that she would even show me such out of the blue. But that is how tainting one's view of someone can occur in my opinion, and it still occurs in many families, relationships, and interpersonal connections of all sorts for defaming reasons.

I do not harbor any unforgiveness toward her, my mother, my father, or others because of what Christ Jesus has done in me and for me. I also have come to understand what God meant when He expressed through the instructions given in Matthew 6:12 that if I do not forgive others, neither their trespasses/debts nor my trespasses or debts will be forgiven. And I know I have wronged some people, whether intentionally or unintentionally. We all need the blood of Christ Jesus for the atonement and remission of our sins because we all have sinned or done things that have wronged someone, in one way or another. Even as I conclude the writing of this book, it was Good Friday yesterday, and tomorrow, most of the country will be celebrating Resurrection Sunday or what most people have traditionally called Easter. So I am amazed at the timing of the completion of the writing of my book during Passover 2023.

I LEAVE YOU WITH THESE PERSONAL WORDS

I say to you, "*Never give up.*" If you are alive and still making it in this life, then *you* have purpose, even if you don't know what it is right now. *You* were spared and did not, by God's grace and mercy, succumb to all that you have been through or that has happened to you. I know that some of you are barely holding on mentally, emotionally, psychologically, and/or perhaps physically, but please don't give up. God knows, sees, and cares for you, even if you feel unloved, have been abandoned, forsaken, or rejected. I personally know and have experienced all those things but was able to, little by little, not just survive but now thrive. And I pray that will be your story too. I am fully aware that things might not be easy as you fight back and go from victim to victor, but I encourage you to stay the course.

Taking one day at a time as well as making one decision at a time has great value in it, especially if you have been running on fumes mentally and emotionally for a long time. Take an assessment of your life, your schedule, how you spend your time, and who you are in a relationship with on a daily or frequent basis. Also, look at what you are listening to and who you are listening to. These things are important, but many people just go along with the flow not understanding that what and who you are listening to and are ingesting, that is, eating but in a different way, can and do greatly affect a person's mood and emotions.

There is a saying which says that a person is what they eat. Most people hear that and automatically think of natural edible food, beverages, and such. But I ask you to consider that this saying also applies to what we are listening to and who we are listening to on a regular basis. I have learned during my transitional coming-up-and-out years from victim to victor that I was weakened, and my resilience/bouncing back from trying challenges was not as strong as it could be because of my diet. Again, I am not just speaking about physical food products, but also the words we speak out and take in via hearing or by reading.

I do know that many people are in families, jobs, and other gatherings where the aura and/or atmosphere can be very negative, but do strive to adjust your immediate involvement with such goings-on if possible. Then begin to seek out positive individuals along your recovery journey, who can motivate you to keep going, inspire you, and speak into your situation, your life, and your future words of life. Words are instruments that hold life and/or destruction within them that can literally influence a person's destiny. These are a few basic adjustments you can begin to immediately make as you bravely and courageously take steps toward becoming the person you were created by God to be. All of us have to start somewhere, whether it is pursuing a college degree, starting a business, or perhaps having a family of your own one day if you find yourself in a single state.

For many years, I tried to not be alone by getting involved with people who I thought loved me because they said they did, only to find out they did not love me. I decided to stop looking for what I needed in another human as I shared earlier in this book, and that was a huge step in my own mental health and emotional health recovery many years ago. I started focusing on self-care, self-compassion, and becoming whole inside and out. I have found that many people think they need to have someone in their life in some way to feel complete. That is not true, even though having a companion, mate, or spouse has great benefits. But if a person is not emotionally or mentally sound themselves because of trauma they have buried and not healed from, then people are susceptible to being attracted and getting in relationships secondary to trauma bonding and other trauma-type compatibility.

PROFESSIONAL CLOSINGS

I would be professionally remiss if I did not mention the following things to you as you begin your trauma recovery journey or continue your journey with a renewed sense of energy. Seek professional therapeutic assistance from a mental health agency and a faith-based entity, such as a local church or community-ran mental health program. There are many community resources allocated toward mental health recovery and good mental health. There are also crisis centers dispersed throughout the United States that have a mission to help people of all ages through emotional or mental health breakdown. The National Suicide Prevention hotline number has been changed to just three numbers, which are 988. There are trained personnel who are skilled and knowledgeable when it comes to intervening as appropriate when a caller finds themselves in a mental health crisis of any sort. You are not alone, and people care about you and your well-being.

I am a faith-based mental health crisis counselor and have been trained both professionally and academically to function in such a capacity, so I am very vested in this line of human services work. And it is not just a form of work for me but a calling. May God bless you and keep you, and that is my prayer. And may God grant you divine peace, accompanied by His unconditional *love* so that you may know, without a doubt, that you matter and that He created you for a great purpose in Christ Jesus's name. Take care, and always remember *you matter*!

REFERENCES

The Amplified Version "Battlefield of the Mind Bible"
Joyce Meyer commentary edition/Copywritten: 2017

ABOUT THE AUTHOR

LaTina Celeste Dorsey, M.A. is a Trauma Specialist, who presently oversees a crisis intervention trauma transitional consulting company Forward Focus & Recovery Consulting LLC. She holds a master's degree in trauma/crisis response, which she attained from Liberty University.

She is presently pursuing her doctorate degree in traumatology and community care counseling. She also attained the professional position as a licensed paramedic, where she functioned for approximately ten and a half years with Baltimore County Maryland Fire Department.

www.ingramcontent.com/pod-product-compliance
Lightning Source LLC
Chambersburg PA
CBHW021147130726
47988CB00004B/1499